Top 10 Mistakes

Agents Make When Marketing Their Real Estate Business

By Michelle Fradella-Barfuss

Dedicated to my loving mother and mentor, Patricia Troup, who left this world too soon in life. You have always believed in me, and have been my guiding force and a true example of strength and purpose.

*~**Michelle***

By Michelle Fradella-Barfuss

Copyright 2014 – Word On The Street Marketing, LLC

All rights reserved. No part of this book may be reproduced or transmitted in any form or by any means, electronic or mechanical, including photocopying, recording or by any information storage and retrieval system, without written permission from the authors, except for the inclusion of brief quotations in a review.

Limit of Liability Disclaimer: The information contained in this book is for information purposes only, and may not apply to your situation. The author, publisher, distributor and provider provide no warranty about the content or accuracy of content enclosed. Information provided is subjective. Keep this in mind when reviewing this guide.

Neither the Publisher nor Authors shall be liable for any loss of profit or any other commercial damages resulting from use of this guide. All links are for information purposes only and are not warranted for content, accuracy, or any other implied or explicit purpose.

Earnings Disclaimer: Any income examples in this book are just that – examples. They are not intended to represent or guarantee that everyone will achieve the same results. You understand that each individual's success will be determined by his or her desire, dedication, background, effort and motivation to work. There is no guarantee you will duplicate any of the results stated here. You recognize any business endeavor has inherent risk for loss of capital.

"The typical result one can expect to achieve is nothing. The "typical" person never gets to the end of this book. The "typical" person fails to implement anything. Thus they earn nothing. Zero. No income. And perhaps a loss of income. That's because "typical" people do nothing and therefore they achieve nothing. Be atypical. Do something. Implement something. If it doesn't work; make a change…and implement that. Try again…try harder. Persist, and reap the rewards."

CONTENTS   Page#

Introduction   7

Mistake #1 - Trying to be Everything to Everyone   15

Mistake #2 – Doing What Everyone Else Does   25

Mistake #3 – Relying Solely on a   31
            Brokerage's Template Website

Mistake #4 – Believing That Just Having a Website   43
            Will Generate Leads

Mistake #5 – Not Targeting Your Market   57

Mistake #6 – Failing to Build Relationships   65
            With Online Visitors

Mistake #7 – Not Having a Call-to-Action in Ads   69

Mistake #8 – Not Using Video   75

Mistake #9 – Forgetting Past Clients   79

Mistake #10 – Not Taking Advantage of Social Media   83
             And Mobile Marketing

Done For You   109

Appendix   113

Introduction

How Hungry Are You?

Often through a career you can find yourself getting fat, happy, and lazy. Let's face it, if you've been in the real estate business for more than 5 years, you've experienced the happy times, when business just flowed and the money kept streaming in. Those are the times when we got comfortable and lazy.

Now think back to the beginning of your real estate career. How was that scenario different?

I remember being a brand new agent. I was hungry. There wasn't a day that went by that I wasn't looking for business – trying to learn everything I could about prospecting, watching the top producers to see what they did. I signed up for all the desk duty I could get, attended every broker tour, and was at the office every day.

Hunger drove me.

So . . . how HUNGRY are YOU?

Or, are you milling around grumbling about how the market has changed, and how business doesn't just fall in your lap anymore? Are you sitting around expecting things to just get better on their own? Are you doing the same old tired marketing that you did back in the "good ole days", the marketing that every other agent is doing, expecting to get results?

The market HAS changed, and so has the way that consumers access information. They're no longer looking in the newspaper, yellow pages, or home buyer magazines. WHY would they even bother, when all they have to do is access their computer, or smart phone, and find out all they want to know?

Did you know that over 90% of all consumers start their home-buying search online, and that newspapers and print publications are struggling to survive?

So . . . what are you doing to get in front of the buyers and sellers searching online, before they find your competition??

And once you have them in your crosshairs, what are you doing to capture them and convert them to closed sales?

Are You Hungry Enough?

In your hunger, are you doing what you can to build a business that YOU run, not one that runs you? One with systems in place that keep attracting business FOR YOU, so you don't have to be hungry again?

Business can change in the blink of an eye. For me, it changed in the passing of the eye of a hurricane.

On August 29th, 2005, Hurricane Katrina literally ROCKED my world. I lived just outside of Picayune, Mississippi, which is 50 miles North of New Orleans and right where the path of the eye of the storm went over. The winds and tornadoes had devastated our area.

The morning after the storm passed, I woke up feeling like my world had ended. I was 6 months pregnant, and scared.

No phone lines, no electricity, no cell towers, no water – all forms of civilization were down.

I put my kids in the car, and we attempted to drive into town. It took a while because of the fallen trees and debris all around.

Then I saw it – my office – looking like a sardine can that someone had pulled the lid back on and discarded on the ground. The rafters and insulation hanging like Spanish moss on an old Oak tree. The desks and files were scattered and wet. Our agents were out of business – - – how was I going to support my family and get my business going again?

After a week of depression and unbearable heat, I drove my family to Memphis, Tennessee (the closest airport that was open), and we flew out to Salt Lake City, Utah, to get away and spend time with friends and family.

I was glad to be out of the heat, and in the refreshing mountains, but I was still worried. How was I going to support my family?

And then . . . the next morning I awoke to my cell phone ringing. It was a buyer looking for a home because they had lost theirs in the storm.

You see, since I began my career in real estate, I have had an online presence. Being the first agent in my market with a searchable website, my online marketing was still working my business for me, even though my physical office was destroyed. The online systems that I had in place kept my business alive.

In fact, in the 2 weeks that I was in Utah, I sold 8 houses! I wasn't even in the same area of the Country, but because my listings were still being advertised online, and I was in a place where my phone would work, the calls came to me.

So what about YOU?

Is YOUR business HURRICANE PROOF?

Ok, so you might not be where hurricanes are a problem. But the real question is – do you have systems in place to put you in front of prospects BEFORE they find your competition?

Does your marketing command attention and drive traffic to YOUR business?

Do you know how to take your marketing efforts online, and stop wasting money on ads that don't work anymore?

Do you know how to leverage your offline and online marketing to capture real leads and get the most return from your advertising dollars?

Do you know how to build a following – a group of raving fans that know, like and trust you, and refer business to you?

If you have said "no" to any of these questions, then you need to listen carefully – I have the answer!

Now I'm not going to fill your head with a lot of fluff about lofty concepts and "ideas". Instead, I'm going to tell you how you can gain access to step-by-step training that will take you to the top of your market.

You will learn:

- How to set up a real online presence (not just a fancy virtual brochure or a cookie-cutter broker site)
- How to set up lead capture (the ones that people will actually fill out, and not the lame forms that most sites contain)
- How to build rapport with prospects for them to get to know, like, and trust you, so YOU will be their agent of choice when the time is right.
- How to drive traffic to your site.
- How to use video in your real estate business.
- How to build a following – to become the **Maven** of YOUR market.

So, let me ask you —

Are You Tired and HUNGRY?

Mistake #1 - Trying to be Everything to Everyone

Every new agent sets out bright-eyed and bushy-tailed, anxious to get all the business they can find.

I know I did.

You come in to the office with high hopes and determination, grasping at any straws that might lead to your first sale.

You take every hour of "floor time" that you can. You bend over backwards to get any whiff of a prospect that you can work with.

I've been there. I get it.

But what if I told you that grabbing everything that comes your way would ultimately make you the LEAST amount of money, in the long run?

What if I told you that the type of prospects you will get, when you are desperate, are the type of clients that will run you ragged, drain your financial resources, and make you start to question your commitment and resolve to having a successful real estate business?

> *"Roughly seventy percent of all real estate agents quit during their first year in business. Oh, they don't always leave right away. Sometimes they hang around, in a state of 'quit', for years, before they finally clean out their desk and walk out the door." - Floyd Wickman, CSP, CPAE Hall of* Fame

Heck, you might even start to consider going back to that J.O.B. (Just Over Broke) that you left when you got your license!

Did you know that 70% of licensed agents quit, after just one year in real estate?

After a full year of slugging it out on the battlefield of business, like a lot of agents, you might be feeling a bit overwhelmed, burned out and somewhat deflated.

What if you could be GUARANTEED that with a few small, simple, and inexpensive changes, and with the right focus, you could have more of what you want, instead of getting more of what you DON'T want?

How would you go about that?

NICHE MARKETING

What is a niche market?

"Niche market" as defined by Webster's New Millennium Dictionary of English, Preview Edition is: "a specialized and profitable part of a commercial market; a narrowly targeted market.

What if there was a way to have people come to you? To close the door on all types of Real Estate and concentrate on one particular type - To have them call you because you are considered an authority in one type of Real Estate?

Some examples of real estate niches are:

- First-time Home Buyer Specialist
- Historic Homes Specialist
- Investment Properties Specialist
- Condo Specialist
- Relocation Specialist
- New Construction Specialist
- Retiree Home Specialist
- Military Moves Specialist
- Green Living Specialist
- Luxury Home Specialist
- Resort and Vacation Homes Specialist
- Short Sale Specialist
- Foreclosure and REO Property Specialist

Gary Gestson is a great example of a niche specialist. When Gary Gestson started in the real estate business, he marketed himself to the masses. He made cold calls, reached out to his sphere of influence, and focused on becoming the go-to guy for real estate in his neighborhood. The problem? "There were thousands of real estate agents in my area who were doing the same thing," says Gestson, a salesperson with Long & Foster Real Estate Inc. in Gaithersburg, Md.

And although he was making a decent living, he wasn't having very much fun. "Selling houses that all look alike quickly became boring to me," he says. Four years later, after creating the Historic Home Team and launching a niche Web site (www.historichometeam.com), Gestson was the top producer at his office. And while other practitioners in his market have struggled with a housing slowdown the last couple of years, he's had a steady stream of business. In fact, 2009 is on track to be a banner year, he says.

> "Having a niche allows me to focus my marketing efforts," he says. "I don't have to reach out as much as I did before. People find me."
>
> Another perk of being a specialist: His clients tend to associate with other historic-home enthusiasts. "If I've got one satisfied customer, I've got 10 referrals waiting," Gestson says. "My clients are very qualified and they're buying something for the long term. They want to work with someone with specialized knowledge." * (Own Your Niche - Realtor.com Magazine July 2009)

The concern that often frightens agents away from focusing on a niche market in their business is this part of the equation. You may say, "I don't want to limit my ability to make money by working with only a few potential customers."

The reality is… when you are operating from the most natural place for you with the people that you are most interested in, the possibilities for financial growth are limitless.

All you need to do is focus on serving your customers well, learn everything you can about your niche, translate your offers into the language of the niche, and be willing to find out how to reach more of these people.

Does this mean that you can never work with buyers or sellers that are not within your niche?

NO. It just means that you focus your time and attention on your specialty, and develop your skills for that niche, so that you magnetically ATTRACT the type of clients you really enjoy working with.

Think about this: Who makes more money - a General Practitioner or a Brain Surgeon?

The Brain Surgeon, right?

Why is that?

They are both doctors.

What makes the difference?

The difference is that one is targeted on a highly specific area of medicine. They have extensive knowledge of that niche, and work that niche daily. The other doctor has a general knowledge of the medical field, and addresses many different problems and many different situations.

So which one do you want to be? The one who tries to service them all, or the specialist who is the rock star in their niche?

Another benefit of working with a specific niche is that your marketing is highly targeted to a specific group of people. When you market to your "ideal client", you spend less money on marketing, and have a greater return on your investment.

Your ads will "speak to" them. Speak to one, not many. They will be attracted to you. Instead of "hope marketing" you will be doing "attraction marketing", and the work is certainly more profitable!

We will talk more about attraction marketing a little later.

So . . . how do you become the "Expert" of your niche? Do you need to know everything there is to know? Do you have to have decades of experience?

The answer is going to surprise you!

No. You don't have to have all the answers and know every detail. You don't have to have decades of experience, and thousands of closings under your belt.

What you DO have to do is assume the role of the professional, study your niche and know the overview, and then enlist the assistance of professionals within your niche that do have the answers and can be trusted affiliates in your business.

These are the professionals in industries related to your niche – lenders, inspectors, attorneys, etc, with whom you can build an alliance with which will give you and your clients the guidance needed.

You take the position of being the publisher of information, collecting knowledge and resources for your niche. You bring the value and resources together, to provide the most comprehensive enlightenment of your choice topic.

You set the stage to be the true expert, because of the value that you provide to your clientele.

As you build rapport with your audience, they will be drawn to you because you "know" their wants/needs.

Mistake #2 – Doing What Everyone Else Does

Advertising -

Open up any real estate magazine, and what do you see . . . The same type of ads throughout.

Over and over again you will find pages of house pictures and listing information, and inevitably at the top of the page, you will see the agent touting how great they are, and how great their brokerage or services are. It doesn't matter where you go in the USA, the ads are the same everywhere.

Do consumers really care how great YOU think you are?
Do they really care how many awards you've received, or how many letters you put behind your name? Do they really know (or care) what all those letters mean?

It's no wonder that consumers think all real estate agents are the same!

What makes you stand out?

What message are you sending to your prospects?

How are you going to get them to connect with you?

The biggest thing that consumers care about is WHAT YOU CAN DO <u>FOR THEM</u>. They subscribe to the channel WIIFM – "What's In It For Me?" If you aren't broadcasting on THEIR frequency, you aren't going to have an audience.

You know the old saying? "People don't care how much you know, until they know how much you care."

And where do you get the most return for your investment? Just because other agents are still using print advertising, does that mean that it's the best way to generate leads for your business? And how do you know who sees your ads? How will you track them?

Over 90% of consumers start their home search online. Do you have the systems in place to attract and capture those leads, to be able to convert them to closed sales (and a paycheck)?

Lead Generation –

When you are in the office, what are you doing? Are you standing around talking to everyone who passes you by?

Are you focused on the menial tasks that get you bogged down for the day, without creating any monetary benefit?

Many agents commonly fall into the trap of conducting their support activities first. These tasks allow them to avoid having to go out and talk to people. They sit in the office and prepare marketing brochures, perfect their listing packets, etc. These ARE things that need to be done, but don't get caught up in thinking that because you are spending so much time IN your business, and are working so hard, that you will be successful. Don't fall into the trap of "busyness" instead of "business".

> *"Action alone does not cause success.*
>
> *Productive action causes success"*

Time block your lead generation, and don't let anything get in that space. Without leads, you have no business. You have to dedicate time to lead generate. Everything else will fall into place.

Blocking time and focusing on what is most important in your business can be hard to do.

> "Salespeople who are not swamped by their work usually had a breakthrough point where they gained a new perspective on time. They reached common conclusions about time before they were able to make a change in how they used their time. These six conclusions are the foundation for everything else:
>
> **1. Life will never settle down until I choose to settle it down.**
> **2. Working is not living.**
> **3. Time is life first, then money.**
> **4. More work usually means less life; less work, more productivity and efficiency, usually means more life.**

5. How I use my time deeply impacts my self esteem, my identity and my fulfillment.

To reclaim your identity and set the stage for regaining control in your days, *you must first understand what is currently defining your identity. Who you are* and *who you are becoming* is foundationally a function of how you are using your waking hours. Most salespeople overlook this in their pursuit of success and become something they never intended to be. What you invest your time in defines who you are. "

- Todd Duncan's Book "*Time Traps*"

Mistake #3 – Relying Solely on a Brokerage's Website

Being listed on your broker's site IS important, to show credibility to prospects (and other agents looking to refer business your way), and to show that you are part of the brokerage. The problem is that too many agents rely on the fact that their company provides a website for them, and they don't do anything else.

Do brokerage websites bring in some business? Yes. But I can assure you that it is not the type of leads that you will get when you have your own web presence online.

What you have to understand about the internet, and search engines like Google, is that they see more than what the consumer sees on the screen. Brokerage templates are all set up to be plug-and-play for their agents. The same basic information is on every page.

Yes, you can go to the trouble of re-writing a lot of what shows up on your site, but the basic HTML language that the search engines read is all the same. Your site looks just the same as any other agent in your office, to the search engines. And since the "Panda Update" that Google put into place in February 2011, meant to stop sites with poor quality content from working their way into Google's top search results, the sites that have duplicate content don't rank in the search engines any more.

What does that mean? It means that because your site looks like all the other agent sites in your brokerage, Google will not rank it, and you miss out on all the prospects searching for property and information in your area.

Many times, the basic background information on the site doesn't even apply to you! Let me show you what I mean. Here is a list of the keywords that I found encoded on a certain company's agent websites (I have removed the brokerage's name, which was repeated several times):

new orleans real estate, new orleans, Metairie, Super search, realestate, realestate, relocate, relocation, homes for sale, open house, orleans, jefferson, st tammany, st bernard, mandeville, covington, hammond, folsom, picayune, laplace, jefferson, ormond, kenner, la, ms, mississippi, gulfcoast, gulf coast, bay st louis, gulfport, biloxi, long beach, condominium, condos, home, house, sell, buy, waterfront, townhouse, relocation parish, corporate relocation, property for sale, property management, realtor, residential, seller, real estate agent, real estate broker, mls, buyer, commercial, french quarter, Garden District, waterfront, listings

As you look through these "keywords" (words that the page is trying to attract traffic for in the search engines), notice that most of these words are generic. If you were to search these terms individually, you would see that they don't pertain directly to real estate, and would produce hundreds or maybe even thousands of sites that would never lead the search engines to a real estate agent, directly.

Also, notice that there are a multitude of areas that are mentioned in the terms. The agent whose website I pulled these from is only licensed in Mississippi. He can't sell in Louisiana, but the Louisiana terms are there as well, because the brokerage covers both states.

So, what should you do?

You should have your own website, run on your own hosting platform, which is niche-specific for your area and expertise. You have to set yourself apart from your competition, and showcase your knowledge and specialization of your niche.

Branding Your Website

Many agents don't understand the intricacies of SEO (Search Engine Optimization), and internet marketing. They believe that if they just have a site, that all the leads will be coming to them.

Another problem is that many agents have been lead to believe that their website domain should be "yourname.com", or some catchy phrase (*be sure to read note from NAR at the end of this chapter).

They fail to do market keyword research to know what people are **actually** looking for when searching online.

So many people start out trying to come up with some cutesy domain name, or something that is "catchy", but they fail to realize that the most amount of traffic to their site will come from search engines, and it's important to make sure those search engines understand what their site is all about, and they find it relevant to what people are searching for.

THE FIRST STEP:

Your first step - **even before buying a domain name** - is to do keyword research and find out what people type in to the search bar, when looking for what you have to offer.

This step is a crucial one.

This domain name will be the heart of your business, and it's going to take some real thinking to see what would work the best.

You see, search engines start reading your site by looking at your domain name, first. What you put here is going to help the search engines determine what your site is about, so you are going to have to include "keywords" in the name which describe the main focus of your site.

Let's say that you are a Realtor in Austin, TX. You are going to be focusing on being a Seller's Agent, listing properties in the Austin area.

Put yourself in the mind of a seller.

What type of terms would they be looking for when searching the internet to find who is selling properties in Austin, TX?

You would probably type something into the search box like "Austin TX Homes For Sale", right? So, wouldn't it make sense to make your domain stand out by being "AustinTXHomesForSale.com". See where I'm going with this? You will need to "load" the domain name with "keywords" that describe what your site is about, and include what people will type into the search bar to find you. This will get you more traffic in the long run.

Now don't go jumping out there and just put in the words that YOU think people are searching for. Make yourself a list of different keywords that would be a possibility for your area.

Once you have a list of words, you are going to first want to test those words out to see if they are ones that are being searched for. You do this by using Google's Keyword Planner tool at **https://adwords.google.com/KeywordPlanner** (you will need a Google account to access this), and typing in the keyword (or series of words – called "search terms") that YOU think is being searched for.

The following page shows a screen shot of the Google Keyword Planner.

Since you have narrowed down the niche that you want to focus on, you can really fine tune the keywords that you will need to be using to generate the highest amount of traffic from your marketing efforts.

Once you have a list of keywords, you need to analyze them. Not every keyword is going to be one you would want to focus on for search engine optimization purposes. Some won't have enough traffic to make them worth the time, and others will have too much competition to give you a reasonable chance to rank.

Choose keywords that make sense, and are the words that your prospects are going to be typing into the search engines to find.

I **DO NOT** suggest using your own name, the name of your brokerage, or the fact that you are a "Realtor®" or real estate agent, within your domain name.

PLEASE NOTE: NAR has established rules on the name "Realtor ®", and it's use.

REALTOR® Trademark/Logo use on the internet

When surfing the Web for real estate homepages, it's quite common to come across sites belonging to REALTORS®. If you are looking to add your own electronic presence on the Internet, it is easy to get caught up in designing your own web page and choosing a domain name which will capture the attention of surfers and make you easily identifiable.

Whether it is the domain name of your home page or other domain names you use to point to your home page, REALTORS® often want to use the REALTOR® marks as part of a domain name or address to distinguish themselves, but they must keep in mind that there are rules governing proper use of the REALTOR® marks that must be adhered to at all times regardless of the media used. These rules are found in the National Association's Membership Marks Manual, a reference manual available on-line at REALTOR.org, explaining proper use of the REALTOR® marks including examples of correct and incorrect uses.

Here is a brief list of the principal rules affecting use of the REALTOR® marks in domain names:

1. The term REALTOR®, whether used as part of a domain name or in some other fashion must refer to a member or a member's firm.

2. The term REALTOR® may not be used with descriptive words or phrases. For example, Number1realtor.com,

numberone-realtor.com, chicagorealtors.org or realtorproperties.com are all incorrect.

3. The term REALTOR® should never be used to denote an occupation or business. Do not combine words like "your," "my," "our" or any descriptive words or phrases between your name and the membership mark. JaneDoeMyRealtor.com and YourChicagoRealtorJohnDoe.com are all examples of improper use.

4. For use as a domain name or e-mail address on the Internet the term REALTOR® does not need to be separated from the member's name or firm name with punctuation. For example, both johndoe-realtor.com and johndoerealtor.com would be correct uses of the term as a part of domain names and jdoe*realtors@webnetservices.com and jdoerealtors@webnetservices.com are both correct uses of the term as part of an e-mail address.

5. The REALTOR® block R logo should not be used as hypertext links at a web site as such uses can suggest an endorsement or recommendation of the linked site by your Association. The only exception would be to establish a link to the National Association's web site, REALTOR.org, or its official property listing site, REALTOR.com. The public has adopted the use of all lower case letters when writing domain names, even those containing trademarks.

> **TIP:**
> *Avoid using dashes in your domain name. Example: If the name www.mytownhomesales.com isn't available and you buy www.mytown-homesales.com, you'll likely be paying for advertising to send YOUR customers to the agent that has the domain name without the dash.*

Therefore, for purposes of domain names and internet addresses only, there is an exception to the rule on capitalization of the term REALTOR® and it may appear in lower case letters. Whether you use traditional print media or the Internet, it is essential to use the REALTOR® marks in accordance with the rules and guidelines of the National Association. The REALTOR® marks should only be used to denote membership in the NATIONAL ASSOCIATION OF REALTORS®.

Used with permission of National Association of REALTORS® 2011.

Mistake #4 – Believing That Just Having a Website Will Generate Leads

When I first started in real estate, back in the late 90's, there weren't very many real estate websites. The ones that were there were basically online brochures.

Today, websites have to be so much more. They need to tell a story, contain useful information for your audience, and highlight you in a way that will showcase you as the "go-to" person, the authority of your niche.

In order to be found by the search engines, your site has to be updated regularly with fresh content, and marketed not only to your prospects, but to the search engines, as well.

There are many ways to market your website in order to attract prospects that will turn into closed sales. It isn't enough to just have an online presence. You have to get the word out there.

> "Content marketing is a method of marketing that uses education as a tool for attracting the attention and interest of your prospects and getting them to identify themselves to you." – David Frey, Author of "The Small Business Marketing Bible"

Driving Traffic to Your Site

Article Marketing

> *Wikipedia Definition:* *Article marketing is a type of advertising in which businesses write short articles related to their respective industry. These articles are made available for distribution and publication in the marketplace. Each article has a bio box and byline (collectively known as the resource box) that include references and contact information for the author's business.*

Well-written content articles released for free distribution have the potential to increase your business credibility within the market. They help greatly in attracting new clients. These articles are often syndicated by other websites, and published on multiple websites.

One of the easiest ways to generate consistent traffic to your website is to set up a series of article campaigns that provide quality content to your target audience, help generate "backlinks" to your website, and draw in traffic from the search engines.

Each article should be between 300 and 600 words in length and provide useful information that your target audience would find appealing.

The greater the number of articles in circulation, the more exposure you will receive, however you always want to focus on producing high quality content, rather than just on the quantity that is being distributed between these networks.

Here are a few of the article publishing sites that are out there:

    http://www.ezinearticles.com
    http://www.Buzzle.com
    http://www.GoArticles.com
    http://www.ArticlesFactory.com
    http://www.WebProNews.com

http://www.ArticleDashboard.com
http://www.ArticlesBase.com
http://www.ArticleWheel.com

There are countless topics that you can cover for content in articles. Think about the questions that people have when buying or selling a house. What type of questions did YOU have when you purchased your first home? What were your worries? These are the type of things you can write articles on that will be of interest to your prospects.

Once you have written your article, you can post it to your website, and post it to article publishing sites that will distribute the articles across the internet, driving traffic back to your site. It's like employing hundreds of people to market for you!

Social Marketing

Are you willing to engage your target audience, and spend some time interacting and socializing in exchange for high quality traffic?

Then Social marketing is for you!

With social marketing, you are able to take a personal approach to connecting with your target audience, and in doing so, you can gain a better feel for what your audience is genuinely interested in and what motivates them into taking action.

The downside to social marketing is that it can be time consuming, as you have to update your profile accounts, status updates and send out messages and broadcasts in order to keep your accounts fresh. The more fresh and relevant you are, the more often your posts will be presented to your viewers. It's extremely important to be providing fresh content on a regular basis, because sites like Facebook and Google+ rank you by the amount of activity you have and social interaction you have with your audience.

There are ways to automate your account updates, like subscribing to free services like Ping.fm (http://www.Ping.fm).

Ping will automatically update multiple social profiles at once, and provide you with the opportunity to schedule future updates, so your accounts can stay active and fresh even when you are on vacation!

If you are interested in using Twitter as part of your marketing campaign, you'll be able to automate your updates as well.

Another service is SocialOomph.com and it not only auto-posts updates to your Twitter feed, but it also enables you to send automatic tweets to those who follow you.

You could send a welcome message thanking the user for following you, and offering them a free report, tutorial, or video series, by directing them to your squeeze page. Or you could simply use this automated feature to establish a relationship with those on your following list, the choice is yours!

Here are the top social media networks that you should consider including in your marketing campaigns:

http://www.Facebook.com

http://www.Linkedin.com

http://www.ActiveRain.com

These are currently the top social sites for real estate agents to engage with their niche, and to connect with other real estate professionals across the Country, that can refer business.

Whenever I am looking for an agent to recommend, these are the first places I look, along with whether or not the agent has their own website and is active in the internet community. I want to refer my clients to those who have the furthest reach, and are active agents.

Video Marketing (See Mistake #8 – Not Using Video)

Facebook Ads

With the popularity of Facebook, almost everyone who has a pulse has access. This is where you can do some of your best advertising, because you can get in front of a VERY targeted audience to promote your business.

With Facebook, you can advertise several ways:

- Graphics
- Posts
- Site Links
- Ads

How to place a Facebook Ad:

1. Click on the "Create an Ad" link.

2. Choose your title, body text and image.

You get 25 characters for a title, 135 characters for the body of the ad and the option of uploading an image.

As such, this is a short ad – so you need to grab attention quickly and call people to action so they click through to your page. Unfortunately, the title is set – it's the title (name) of your Business Page. So that means you just have the body copy (135 characters) to get people to take action.

Once you've filled in your ad and uploaded your image, then…

3. Click "Continue."

4. Complete your "targeting" information. Who is your target market? This is where you decide who gets to see your ads. Be specific as possible to generate the best results. This is where you choose who your ad will be posted to on the side of their timeline and wall. It's very important to be niche-specific when setting up these ads, because the more targeted you are, the better results you will get, for less money.

5. Click "*Continue*."

6. Choose your budget. This is where you choose when to start your ad, on what dates your ad should appear, our daily ad budget and whether you want to pay per click or per impression.

Tip: You may want to start off paying per click – that way, you are only paying for those people who are most interested in your ad. That is, you're only paying for people who've qualified themselves.

Ultimately you'll want to test both kinds of ads to see which one brings you the best results and the most Fans.

Make your choices and...

7. Click *"Review Ad."* Now you come to the place where you can review everything, from your ad to your budget. If you see any problems, click *"edit ad."* Otherwise, fill in your credit card information and choose *"place order."*

That's it! Now just test different ad copy, ad formats and targeting to see which produce the best results for you.

Direct Mail

These are postcards, letters, flyers and advertisements that you send out to your SOI (sphere of influence), and your target market. Do not discount what seems to be an old way to market. Many agents want to focus on just email marketing, but with the spam filters that most internet providers have in place, your message can be seen as a promotion, and sent to the spam box where consumers may never see your message.

Direct mail is not antiquated. It is reliable, it is effective and it can be inexpensive as well, as long as you are focusing on a niche market, and not trying to blast it out everywhere, to everyone.

The key with direct mail is frequency. People may not be ready for your message right now and that's why you need to have repetition and follow-up.

> We live in a time where professionals everywhere are suffering from inbox overload, and with 300 billion messages sent each day, that is hardly surprising. So in a time where every business everywhere is sending email after email, it makes a nice change for a direct mail to land upon a CEO's desk on a Monday morning.

In fact, some may call it a novelty to receive an interesting piece of direct mail - you instantly stand out from the plethora of emails. And given the fact that printing costs have fallen drastically, you can send out something a little different from your competitors without having to contend with an ever dwindling marketing budget.
("Direct Mail: It's Not Dead!" by Suzanne Stock)

Keep in mind that any marketing that you do should involve "direct response marketing", that includes a call-to-action, and a reason for the prospect to respond.

See *Mistake #7 – Not Having a Call-to-Action in Ads* on page 57.

Free Reports

These are offers to reports that prospects can receive via email, that are sent out automatically. These reports should contain your contact and information that will lead them back to your website.

See Mistake #6 – *Failing to Build Relationships with Online Visitors* on page 53.

Pinging

Pinging notifies the search engines when your site has new content. This is extremely important, because in order for your site to remain relevant in the eyes of the search engines, you have to continually update and create fresh content.

When the new content is created, you have to notify the search engine bots to come back to your site and re-index what you have. This can be done manually, or through a plugin on your Wordpress site that does it automatically for you, every time you publish a new post.

NOTE: *Please be sure to check with your State Real Estate Commission, your local Board and Brokerage/Franchise to insure that you are in compliance with requirements set by these organizations in regard to what MUST appear on electronic and print communications.*

Mistake #5 – Not Targeting Your Market

In this section you're going to get to know the most important person in your business universe (and that person ISN'T YOU).

He or she is most responsible for transforming your current life into your ideal life.

When you really appreciate their importance, you realize that most real estate agents haven't really begun the real work they need to do to get their business going.

Of course, we're talking about your ideal client. And the purpose of this section is to help you know them better than your competitors do. In fact, you should know them better than anyone else you know.

Remember, they are the ones who are going to give you the money you need to have the business of your dreams, a business that delivers to you your ideal life.

Knowing your ideal prospects and clients will:

- Dramatically decrease the cost of acquiring new clients causing your business to grow faster and be more profitable at the same time.
- Make everything you do on a marketing level more effective, more certain to succeed, and more profitable immediately.
- Assist you in creating marketing messages that are sure to succeed because they address the needs and subconscious desires of your prospects and clients.
- Make bonding with your prospects and clients a cinch
- And so much more…

> "To get everything YOU want in life, just help SOMEONE ELSE get what they want - FIRST!"
> - Jeffrey Gitomer

Knowing Who Your Ideal Clients Are... And What They Really Want

The Core Complex of your ideal customer addresses the emotions, attitudes, and aspirations that drive their buying behavior. In order to construct your clients' core complex you first must discover their beliefs, feeling and desires. Know your ideal clients' frustrations, fears, dreams, desires, and problems. Remember, you're designing a business that'll deliver to you your ideal life. Everything you want can happen for you, but your business will only be able to do that if you build your business around what your clients really need. The only way to know that is to know them really well. That only comes from doing the research and thinking necessary.

> "I do not believe in 'generic' persuasion. In fact, my contention is that truly understanding the targeted prospect/customer is more important than any other element in a marketing success."
> – *Dan Kennedy*

Identifying My Ideal Client

Beliefs – These are the beliefs of my ideal client:

Fears – These are the fears of my ideal client:

Desires – These are the true desires of my ideal client:

Now that you are armed with knowledge about your ideal client, you need to create marketing materials that will attract these types of clients to you, with videos, articles, and advertisements that address their deepest concerns, needs and fears.

You want to match the message with those you want to attract to your business.

Mistake #6 – Failing to Build Relationships with Online Visitors

How do you know when a prospect has been to your website?

Do you offer anything of value that they would be interested in exchanging their email address for?

What would your business look like if the prospects that come to your site would give you their email address, so you could send them something of value and start to build rapport with them?

Your site should be more than a place for them to search properties for sale. They can get that anywhere these days. IDX search is great, but it's not special any more. Real estate agents no longer hold the ticket to the holy grail (properties for sale). Consumers can find that out anywhere, so what will bring them to YOUR site, and what will keep them there?

You need to address the concerns, needs and fears that you uncovered in the last exercise. Your site should offer them special reports, videos, tutorials about the things that matter most to them.

Offer sellers something they need to know to get the most money when selling their house.

Offer buyers the information they need to make the best buying decisions for their money.

Train them on the process. Let them know what they need to know, and answer the most common questions they ask when you work with them. This saves you time (because they won't need to ask when they are with you), and it sets you apart as an authority on the things they are concerned about. This elevates you in their mind to an expert.

Most people that start an online property search may be months away from actually taking that step.

Being able to connect with them, and start to build rapport with them over time, will assure that you are first on their minds when the time does come for them to move forward. This sets you apart from all your competition, because you demonstrate care about what they need, your knowledge about your market, and you become a trusted friend and advisor.

Another way to capture leads on your site is to offer a membership to a special online community, within your website, where they can go to find out information. In order to do this, you need special software on your website that will lock certain pages and information that can be accessed only when they have joined your site, giving you their email address.

You can also set up special campaigns that will collect their information, and automatically send out the reports, videos, etc, that you will send them.

These campaigns should also have a follow up series that will keep in touch with them over time.

Through a special program we offer, **MyInstantAgent™**, you can have specific campaigns set up for Expireds, FSBO's, Open Houses, etc, that will collect the leads and send out material using multiple channels of communication including email, text messages, voicemail, CD's and greeting cards. This system works in coordination with software called **Instant Customer** and contains all of the special reports, text messages, and tools that you need so you don't have to come up with them all on your own.

It's a copy/paste system to plug in to Instant Customer, that puts your marketing and follow up on autopilot. For more information about that system, be sure to check out **http://myinstantagent.com**.

Mistake #7 – Not Having a Call-to-Action in Ads

Any advertising that you do that is not targeted to your niche audience, and doesn't call your prospect to an action which will enable you to communicate with them, is money wasted.

You have to have a purpose in all your marketing. Your purpose is to gain the lead. You cannot do that if you market like the every other real estate agent out there.

Create a Lead Magnet

Once you have established who your Ideal Client is, the next step, is to create a "lead magnet." A lead magnet is a piece of content that you either give away or sell that is educational, but leads your prospect to inquire about your services.

Your lead magnet could be a written special report, a book that you wrote, a video series, an audio CD, a DVD.

The topic of your lead magnet should be something that resonates with your ideal client. Come up with the #1 concern of your ideal client, and then develop a report about that concern.

Video is my first choice because it's easy to consume, it has a higher perceived value and because people are watching you on a video setting, it increases your "likeability" factor and establishes you as an authority figure. You could create a video series that discusses the prospects concerns, or walks them through the process of listing or buying a home with you.

Lead Capture Page

Once you have your "lead magnet" created, you will need to have a way to introduce and offer the magnet to your audience. This is a page that has a headline to attract attention to what you are giving away, and a section where they can input their name and email address, in order to receive the gift.

A Lead Capture Page is also known as a Landing Page, or a "Squeeze Page". It is a page for your prospect to "land" on, that offers them something of value or interest, in order to obtain their email address. It is a simple page with your offer, and an opt-in box to submit their email address, to be able to access what you are offering (ie. free report, free video, free newsletter). If you have anything more on the page than this, your page will not convert well, and will confuse your prospects because there is no clear call-to-action.

Here is an example of a landing page:

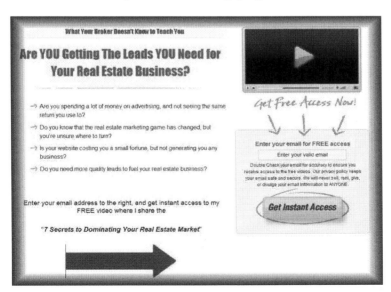

Landing Page Basics

Here are some tips on creating the best landing pages for your business.

- Make sure everything shows "above the fold"
- Create an "attention-grabbing" headline
- Use ultra-specific, benefit-driven bullet points
- Clearly define the "call-to-action"

What I mean by making sure your information is "above the fold" is that you need to make sure everything shows up in the browser window, and your prospects don't have to scroll down any.

You also need to make sure you use an attention grabbing headline that will keep the prospect's attention and make they want to read more.

When you are developing the body of your page, use specific benefits that your prospect will obtain when opting in to get what you are offering. It HAS to be focused on your prospect, and NOT on you.

And lastly, be sure that your "call-to-action" is easy to see, and that you have arrows or other descriptive graphics that draw their eye to the opt-in box, so they have no doubt what you want them to do.

There are many ways to create a landing page. You can use an HTML editor to create a simple page that includes the information you see in the example on the previous page, or you can use a plugin that automates a page on your Wordpress blog.

Tying It Together

In order to have a spot on your landing page where your prospects can enter their email address, and it will be loaded directly into your Autoresponder Account, you will need to get a code that is generated automatically to be input in to the page. Most autoresponder programs, like AWeber, Constant Contact, or MailChimp, to name a few, have step-by-step directions on how to get the code on your page.

Now that you have your lead capture system set up, you will need to create advertising that will announce your gift that they can receive, and the address of the page to go to in order to download that gift.

Mistake #8 – Not Using Video

Did you know that YouTube is the 2nd ranking search engine, next to Google? People use YouTube.com to search for topics they are interested in, to find out more information.

Google loves video, and video actually ranks higher in the search engines than regular websites. So why not use this form of attraction marketing for your business?

If you've been following along, and doing your homework, you have created a list of article topics that prospects in your niche would be interested in (see "Article Marketing, page 32). Now take that list and turn those articles into videos that people can watch to get the information. Most people prefer to watch a video, versus reading an article.

Creating videos is not hard. There are many great tools out there today that you can use to make your video. You can be on-screen (video of you talking), or you can create a slideshow using some of the following tools:

- PowerPoint (Microsoft)
- ScreenFlow (Apple)
- VideoScribe (Sparkol.com)
- Animoto (Animoto.com)
- Prezi (Prezi.com)

Content is far more important than having professional-level production, so don't stress about having a fancy camera and editing software. Instead, start with what you already have.

Do you own an iPhone? Most smartphones take great video, so use the gear that you already own, and then improve from there. Or better yet, use the images and video footage you already have to create an **Animoto video**.

Once you create the presentation, you can walk through it, while narrating, and using a screen recording tool like Camtasia (or their free version – Camstudio).

Then just edit the video you recorded, using a video editing program like:

- Windows Movie Maker
- iMovie (Mac)
- Sony Vegas Video Editor

- Camtasia
- Windows Live
- Adobe After Effects
- Pinnacle Studio HD

With these programs you can edit out your bloopers, and add in background music, graphics, and special effects.

Once you create your video, you can upload it to video hosting sites, such as:

- YouTube
- Vimeo
- Viddler
- Metacafe
- Blip.tv
- Yahoo Video

These are just a fraction of the sites that are available to upload your videos to. The more places you put your video (provided that you put a link to your website in the description of the video), the more "backlinks" you will have back to your main website, which will drive prospects in, and will push your website ranking up in the search engines.

You can then embed your video directly on your website, or blog, and send it out to social media such as Facebook, Twitter, etc.

Our society is focused on video, and those that appear in video set themselves apart from their competition because they develop a celebrity following.

Video actually pushes you to an authority position in your prospect's mind, and elevates their trust.

Mistake #9 – Forgetting Past Clients

One of the biggest mistakes the agents make is forgetting these priceless gems! If you want to keep your business building itself, you have to keep the relationships you build with clients along the way going. These people are the biggest asset of your business.

You have already spent a wealth of time and money to get their attention, and have shown them what you can do. Just because the sale is over, doesn't mean you have to ditch them.

These can be a goldmine to your business, if you play your cards right!

What can you do to keep the relationship going?

Here are some examples:

- Keep them updated on the market, and the values of their neighborhood.
- Notify them of special events in their local area.
- Send them home maintenance tips each season.

- Invite them to a special customer appreciation dinner.
- Send them your monthly newsletter.
- Send them a card on the anniversary date of the purchase of their home.
- Mail them a birthday card.
- Acknowledge when you see special events happening in their lives (this is where social media can help out).
- Enroll them in a special referral group.

I'm sure that you can come up with other ways to keep in contact with these special people. Instead of rushing out to look for the next NEW deal, be sure to continue the relationships that you have cultivated, and reap the benefits of future business through referrals and repeat purchases.

One of the most gratifying experiences is to have one of your past clients refer a friend or family member to you, and it's always a great perk when they call you up a few years down the road and they want to do business with you again!

Failing to keep up with past clients is one of the biggest ways agents leave money on the table. They are so focused on finding new business, they forget the ones that they worked so hard to obtain before. How many additional sales could YOU do each month, if your past clients willingly referred business to you on a regular basis, because you have kept the lines of communication open?

Mistake #10 – Not Taking Advantage of Social Media and Mobile Marketing

Why Social Media?

Simply put: Social media is starting to become a very powerful force in how Google is determining what is relevant online. The Internet is full of bots, scammers, and article spinners, and many links out there are links to irrelevant or otherwise spammy articles.

Social media, however, does the vetting by itself: Users of social media sites aren't going to share spammy links with each other, they're going to share real content. As a result, Google has realized that indexing and calculating relevancy from social media is very beneficial, since social media (in general) has real people posting real content, content that was valuable enough to warrant a "hey, check this out" from one person to another.

Some of us have been trying to avoid social media for one reason or the other; privacy, general lack of interest, or whatever other reason you may have avoided it thus far. The statistics on social media and Internet marketing, however, can't be denied: Gen Y have outnumbered Baby Boomers, since 2010. More than 96% of them have joined a social network. These are the people that look, and by ignoring the social media segment you're basically ignoring their primary mode of access.

- the average time on Google is three minutes. The average time on Facebook is thirteen minutes.
- In September 2012, Facebook reached over 1.11 billion users, and it's growing exponentially every day! To put that into perspective, that means Facebook has more users than the US population; this is very important in terms of saturation.

What these statistics should show you is that social media is a very, very powerful force in today's cultural mindset, and it's only getting stronger. Social media is here to stay, and more and more people every day are joining it and receiving advice from their friends and family about great stories or services that they received.

Google has been taking notice of that and responding accordingly, and so should you. In this chapter, we're going to take a look at social networks and your strategy for them: we're going to figure how just to approach these social media websites and use them to help Google notice you!

The Social Networks

In the social media game, there are currently three huge players that we're going to focus on: Facebook, Twitter, and LinkedIn. This isn't to say you should ignore the other social media networks out there; they're still important, and in fact location-based social media like Foursquare and Facebook Places are very useful too. You may want to have a presence in those, and other minor social networks as well, like YouTube (as we'll be discussing later in this book), Google+, etc.

For the core of our marketing strategy, however, we're going to focus on the big three. This focus will give you the most coverage and best ROI in terms of time spent on marketing, and so it's how we'll proceed!

Facebook

Facebook's the biggest social media in the room, the 800-pound gorilla; everybody knows and uses it, so you're going to need to capitalize on that. The first thing you should have is a business page, and so we'll take a look at how to create one and how to link it into your overall Internet marketing strategy.

TIP:

Many of you will be scared of Facebook's privacy implications. It's very important to note that your business fan page is NOT your personal page. It's not connected to your personal page, it's not the same thing as your personal page, and nothing you post on your personal page will appear on your business page or vice versa. They are completely separate entities! For those you of you resisting joining Facebook / are afraid your business page will expose your personal page, fear not: none of your personal information will go on your business page, and your privacy is safe.

Your Facebook Business Page

A business page (once called a 'fan page'), quite simply, represents your business. Facebook business pages can have dynamic pages that offer info about your business- you're going to want someone to build a custom iframe on the landing page for your business page; your web developer or webmaster should be able to do this pretty easily. When new visitors come to the business page they will see the information in the iframe, which will be an opt-in box and benefit information; this will be very similar to the calls to action you have on your main website- such as a report about the "Top 10 Mistakes Sellers Make When Selling Their House".

The great part of this business page is that you're adding new clients onto an email marketing list through a social media channel. It's a very organic way of getting warm leads and targeted marketing.

While you're creating your Facebook business page, don't forget about your Facebook Places page as well. The location-based aspect of this is really attractive, especially because of the proliferation of mobile phones. More and more people are buying smartphones and more and more things are going mobile; with a Places page, people can check in and see what's around them, and you can offer specials through this mode of delivery. At least get on this radar, but you can take it further- be creative! Combine things like your Business page and Places page, and figure out ways to synergize the two to make an effective marketing vehicle!

The most important thing to know about social media in general; all of these things can be linked together in different ways. There are so many options for managing Business pages and Places pages that it's vital you have a professional who knows how to set up social media correctly. Barring that, you need to get online and do some extensive research into establishing the proper social media channels; it's not something you can just slap together quickly.

Once you've got your Business Page and Places set up, it's time to move on!

Twitter

Twitter—one of the newest social networks out there, and perhaps one that inspires the most reluctance to join. It's been much vilified by the media and our peers, but the fact remains that Twitter is important: it's the most open social network out there.

In fact, this is the whole reason Twitter is so important. Every single tweet (a "tweet" is what each individual Twitter post is called) is indexed by Google.

Other social networks, like Facebook and LinkedIn, need a username and password to see most of their content; with Twitter, there's no requirement to log in to see individual tweets. What this means is that Google can index all the tweets out there, and this means that Twitter informs Google page rankings enormously; Google is using people's tweets to help gauge the importance of pages all around the Internet.

Pages with lots of links from Twitter, for example, are going to increase its importance: you don't want to be spammy, but you do want to take advantage of this fact.

That's the basis of most of your Twitter interaction, when it's all said and done: taking advantage of Twitter's ability to generate constant content without coming across as being spammy. You can't just blast out links to your blog articles all day; a stream of useless / irrelevant content from you (or rehashed content) isn't going to help you to increase your page rank.

You are going to want to create a bunch of tweets about local things like events as well as topical content like minor changes, changes that would be important or useful for people to know.

Your tweets are going to be composed of similar content to your blogs, except shortened down to the 140 character limit per tweet, and sent out once or twice a day.

This may seem as daunting as the blogging, especially considering the daily frequency of the tweets.

The truth be told, however, 140 characters is not that much at all, and you don't have to sit by the computer and send them out one by one; there are tons of websites / programs that let you schedule tweets, including

- HootSuite (**http://hootsuite.com**),
- SocialOomph (**http://www.socialoomph.com**),
- and more

You can sit down for an hour and write enough tweets for a week or two, schedule them, and forget about them until the next week when you sit down to write some more!

But don't be tempted just to tweet an exact duplicate of your blog posts or articles!

Your tweets should be on the same content as your blog posts, but they shouldn't be copied and pasted straight from the blog.

What you can do, however, is to link back to your blog from your tweets: in fact, this is not only permissible but encouraged!

There are many, many plugins for countless blogging platforms that enable you to automatically send out a tweet with a link to your blog post every time you post a new blog post.

Take advantage of that to generate links to your blog posts—that's not spammy since it's only once or twice a week, and it's a great tool for slowly and steadily creating links back to your blog. There are also plugins for Facebook as well—make sure when you post a blog, it's getting automatically posted to your Twitter and Facebook page!

LinkedIn

In the social media circles, LinkedIn is often completely overshadowed by its bigger social media cousins Facebook and Twitter. It is instead regarded as just a professional or resume-sharing site and nothing more; this is a big misstep for many, as LinkedIn is an enormous cash cow if used properly.

For starters, LinkedIn itself is no slouch in terms of financial recognition; now publicly traded (LNKD), Linked In has a market cap of $8-$10 billion (or $70-$100 per user)—making it a very formidable, fast-growing contender in the social media sphere.

Additionally, LinkedIn has an added attraction to us that isn't related to its market share.

Because of LinkedIn's status as a site for professionals and resume-swapping, the average LinkedIn user is far more likely to be a potential client because of the means / motive aspect we described earlier with Facebook:

1. Over one fifth of users are Middle Management level or above
2. Almost 60% have a College or Post Grad degree
3. Average Household Income is $88,573.
4. All of these numbers are higher than published statistics for Wall Street Journal, Forbes, or BusinessWeek.

Put simply, LinkedIn users are wealthier and have more need for services and non-useful demographics, like teenagers, aren't crowding the LinkedIn user space to post pictures of their friends and pets.

LinkedIn is composed of your potential clients interacting with each other, looking for professionals and just waiting to be introduced to your business.

Press Releases

This isn't really social media, but we're going to incorporate it into this section because it deals with controlling a message that goes out and can get shared and receive comments; in a sense, the medium of the Internet itself is social. PR is also one of the few places where Google expects duplicate content; the more duplicated/shared the press release is, the more important the content must be.

15 Great Press Release Ideas:

1. Someone in your company is speaking at an industry conference, local chamber, rotary club, etc.
2. You hire someone new into your team.
3. You join an association (local or national)
4. You start offering a new service or feature.
5. New office space or additional office added.
6. Successful client -- create a Case Study and send out press release.
7. Awards received or recognition from local or national industry or association.
8. Employee or officers named to charity benefit or non-profit board.

9. Large sponsor of a charity benefit.
10. Your product and services tie into a big current event news item (new government law, flood insurance, mortgage rates, etc.).
11. Launch of a new website.
12. The release of your special report.
13. Notify the public about attending real estate related courses, conventions, or workshops that apply to your business to show you value education and its importance.

There are both paid and free press sites out there; the paid press sites are worth the money sometimes because they go out to Associated Press and other big name news wires, like Yahoo and Google News. The more that your story gets out there, the more possibility it is that it could get picked up; a local paper could see that press release and pick up the story, for example, and that's a great thing to take advantage of.

The problem of duplicate content goes out the window because duplicate content is expected in press releases, and often the big names, like Associated Press and Reuters, even source duplicate content!

GOOGLE+:

What makes Google+ different from Facebook, Linkedin, Youtube and Twitter?

There are many social networks, but let's focus on the big 4 Facebook, Linkedin, Youtube and Twitter. Understanding how these sites operate helps explain Google+

Youtube – I make a video. You search for it and can watch, share, or comment on my video. As a search based network this is the most open network of them all. Few people use the subscribe function as a social element.

Linkedin – Use to be: Here is my resume, please hire me – Now is: I need a job, I collaborate with my colleagues & vendors to learn and grown in groups, and I get / answer questions. The most closed network of the 4, you must know my email, already have worked with me, or be in a group with me to connect.

Twitter – I can push information out to many people and this information can be spread quickly. Google indexes this network, which is a bonus. As many people as are on Twitter can follow my updates. You can follow me and I do not need to follow you. Information is sent out in short bursts, and interaction takes place both on Twitter (in a short conversation style) and off Twitter (follow this link to see this video, read my blog, etc)

Facebook - The current king of social media. Facebook is about "friendships". You and I must mutually like each other to share information. I can post information with hopes that this information is seen on your News Feed. There is no guarantee my information will be seen by my friends. Facebook controls information and uses an algorithm called 'Edge' to determine what information they believe I want to see. There is a great business component with Business Pages (formally fan pages).

Google+ What makes you so different?

From a big picture Google+ is all about connecting all of your computer uses both online and offline in one place. We are talking cloud on a major scale. We are talking about your documents, spreadsheets, applications, videos, everything being available in one location and everything being one click from something you can share.

This brings us to the MAJOR DIFFERENCE of Google+:

I can share all my information from my blog to my expense report, but I don't want to share everything with the world. My mom does not need to know about everything about work and my clients don't want to know about my personal life.

Google+ plus has created a revolutionary function called CIRCLES. Circles control both the stream of information out and in. People you connect with are organized into different circles.

How do Circles work and why are they important?

1) You can create any circle you want. Examples of circles include: Following, Friends, Best Friends, Real Estate Agents, Clients, Vendors, Very Smart Marketing People, Funny Peeps, Family, etc.

2) The people you connect with can be in multiple circles. Some people that are Very Smart Marketing People are also my Friends

3) I can choose to send information to one, or more, circles. This information will appear on their wall or can be sent as a message. The great thing is if I share something with my client circle only then no one else sees that post on their feed. Maybe we just got back from a family vacation and I want to share the photos with my family and friends but do not want to bother my vendors, clients, and the general public with the images.

4) I can choose to see information from one or more circles in my feed. Instead of being told what content an algorithm thinks I would like to see, I can choose my content feed based on my circles. This allows me to quickly and easily navigate from one set of feeds to the next. Since you can have people in multiple circles, I know that I am seeing what I want from whom I want.

Here are a few other features to Google+

- Multiple Video Chat. Google+ will allow you to connect with up to 10 people on live video chat at the same time. The feature is smooth and audio is good. A real great way to connect with people for virtual meetings. The best part of this feature is the person talking gets the main screen.

- Larger image and video display on the wall. When you post a video or images they are about 3 times larger on the wall when compared to Facebook.

- Easy navigation to all of Google's functions. While on Google+ you can search the web, see your gmail messages, and access your Google Documents.

- Simple share option. This is very similar to Facebook Google+ uses both a +1 button (similar to Facebook's like) and a "share this post" option.

- 1 click and you can add someone. If you see a name in a post, find someone in your friends feed, or stumble upon someone of interest you can add them without navigating to their page. This is very convenient. When you hover over their name you a box appears giving you the option to add them to a circle.

Setting up Google+ is simple. Similar to other social media outlets, there is an area for information about you, pictures, website URLs, and basic data. As always, only share what you are comfortable sharing. Make sure your about me section has benefits to working with you and keywords for your industry. Like Linkedin there is a title are that you should also include keywords about your area of practice.

The difficult part about social media is that it is rapidly changing.

Just The Facts:

- Social media is one of the most important forces in marketing today: it can't afford to be ignored, and you need to set up strategies for dealing with it.

- The three biggest social media players right now are Facebook, Twitter, and LinkedIn: you need to have pages for them and have a system set up on your blog that pushes blog updates to the respective social networks.

- Google+, though relatively new, is rapidly growing: make sure to incorporate it into your marketing strategy!

- Press releases are an extremely important part of your online marketing strategy, so much so that you should have your marketing business do it for you and cut down on the immense amount of time you're spending on it.

- Social media is rapidly changing, and no single strategy will stay effective forever; make sure to keep yourself updated to stay ahead of the game!

Using Mobile Apps In Your Business

With today's technology, and people's short attention spans, it's extremely important to be where your prospects are.

In order to keep in front of clients and prospects, you need to be visible in the palm of their hand - - - on their mobile device. You run a business, and YOUR business should have a mobile app that prospects can use on the go, directly from their iPhone, Android, iPad, etc.

This is where a Mobile App comes in. This is where you can provide not only immediate service (like the ability to search properties for sale), but long term service as well, such as keeping them abreast of local events, tips and tricks, area information, school information, etc.

Please do not mistake a mobile app for a mobile-ready website.

You SHOULD make sure that your websites are mobile-friendly, meaning that they are easily readable from any mobile device, but a mobile app is a free-standing software that your prospects download. It gives your prospect more flexibility in the things it offers.

Being able to search for properties on their phone gives clients the flexibility of being able to look something up as they drive around the area. When they do that from YOUR mobile app, they have all your contact information right in front of them, and can connect with you by the push of a button.

Your app should also make it possible for you to be able to send them new listings, new area features, announcements, and many other items that will keep you in front of them during the sale process. Once they purchase a property, you will still be able to stay in front of them because you are providing unique services directly to their device.

When you are the go-to person with the answers, you become their hero. Phone number directories for utilities, schools, area restaurants, municipal services, contractors, etc, are much needed once a person purchases a new home.

You can also partner with local attractions, restaurants, gift shops, contractors, and advertise their services on your app, and send out valuable coupons from those partners, that your prospects and clients would be interested in.

The best time to be in front of someone is when they are at that moment of decision when they want to buy or sell. Being in front of past clients when they are talking to friends and family who express an interest in purchasing also gives you an edge to be the one that they refer their friends and family to.

You cannot be the forgotten agent, when you are providing continuous value, even after the sale.

This can help you keep the relationship going.

For an example of what a mobile app for real estate can do, be sure to check out our Mobile App site: **MyLocalREApp**™ at **http://mylocalrealestateapp.com**. There you will find a video that walks you through what a mobile app can do for your real estate business.

Done For You

The last thing you're going to need is a workforce. Let's face it, you didn't go to real estate school, pass the exam, and build your business just so you could spend 11 hours a day uploading videos, submitting listings to directories, and designing websites.

Now we really wish we had better news for you, but finding competent people to do this work for you is not easy. Most web designers are broke, they know nothing about marketing, and many don't have any clients outside of your local city, and yes, they often live in their parent's basement. This is not the kind of person you can trust with your marketing budget so be thorough in deciding who to invest with.

We get asked all the time where to find a good marketing resource, and our answer is that every time we find one who knows what they are doing (they are rare), we hire them to work on our team.

So How Can I Get All Of This Done?

First, by now you'll agree, local web marketing is probably the most time-sensitive, urgent issue on your calendar right now. It doesn't seem like it at the moment, but when you look back on this book 6-18 months from now, you will probably wish that you had a time machine to get you back to this day.

The local Internet marketing door is WIDE open right now, but it is closing fast…and we would not want you to miss out on securing the financial future of your business just because you were out working with clients and closing deals.

On the other hand, it's very difficult to find good people to help you with your online presence. Most web designers are flakes. Even if they knew how to put up a good site, it doesn't mean they can get you on page #1 of Google multiple times.

REAL ESTATE MAVEN™ PROGRAM

Putting this all together, to work for you, can be very time consuming. Our **Real Estate Maven™** Program may be what you are looking for.

Word on the Street Marketing, LLC offers a turn-key, 100% "Done-For-You" service which means you send us your business contact information, we get specific information about your real estate market and your niche, and we can do the rest. You don't have to spend the long hours learning website design, and marketing techniques. We have a complete system of Website Marketing, Mobile Marketing, and Social Media Marketing that can be tailored to fit your business needs.

The purpose of the **Real Estate Maven ™** Program is created to set you apart as the celebrity and authority in your niche market. YOU become the Maven of your market.

When you are the Maven of your market, you don't have to chase business any longer. Everything is specially designed to elevate you to an expert in your industry. Someone that people will be attracted to, and want to do business with.

If you feel that your business is ready to take its marketing to the next level, please check out our website at :

MavenOfRealEstate.com

APPENDIX A: GLOSSARY

ANALYTICS: Analytics are technical measures you can take to see what happens with visitors on your website: how long they stay, what they click, how many of them return to the website, and statistics of that nature. One of the best analytic software packages out there currently is Google Analytics, which is also free.

AUTORESPONDER: An autoresponder is a system put in place to automatically respond to communication initiated by a potential client, usually via email. Autoresponders can range from simple to extremely complex, and can either send just one generic email or choose from dozens of templates depending on the form used by the potential client or the information provided to the autoresponder by the potential client.

BLOG: Originally an abbreviation of the term "web log", it has now come to mean a type of website (or part of a website) that is frequently updated with new content and has many interactive options for users to leave comments and otherwise participate; many blogs are powered by software explicitly designed to make this frequent updating an easier and smoother process, like Wordpress or Typepad.

CALL TO ACTION: Content on a website or other method of communication that appeals to the reader to contact the business.

CRM: An acronym for "Customer Relationship Management". In the context of Internet marketing, it most often refers to the software put in place that manages clients and potential clients of the business; names, locations, likes, dislikes, needs, and other information that the business may find relevant.

DIRECTORY: In the sense of Internet marketing, a website or part of a website whose purpose is to list businesses. Many of these, like Yelp, Merchant Circle, or CitySearch, also contain reviews of businesses that are often user-generated and submitted.

DUPLICATE CONTENT: Identical content that appears on multiple websites. Search engines have created ways of detecting this and often have algorithms that even detect if the content has just been altered slightly; content that has just be altered slightly and is still virtually identical to the original content will still be flagged as duplicate content by many search engines.

E-COMMERCE: The buying and selling of products and services over the Internet.

FACEBOOK: A social networking site that is currently the most popular in the world; it allows users to network with each other and socialize, including sharing photos, thoughts, status updates, and wall posts with each other.

FACEBOOK PLACES: A specific segment of the social networking site Facebook that allows users to see local spots around them as well as update their location in real-time from mobile phones or other means, allowing other users to see where they are at any given time.

GEOLOCATION: In Internet marketing and SEO, a term used to describe location-specific information; normally city and state for most local businesses.

GOOGLE MAPS: A part of Google's website that primarily deals with maps and navigation. One of the features of Google Maps is the ability for local businesses to list themselves on it, and the local search return feature was originally a part of this system. Google later integrated it into the main search system when it proved to be popular.

GOOGLE PLACES / GOOGLE + LOCAL: A part of Google's website that allows a business to have a specific page dedicated to them. It often hooks in with their location on Google Maps, and it features user-generated reviews of the business as well as links to other directories and review sites.

IP ADDRESS: A unique number that identifies a computer on a network.

KEYWORD: A term that a user searches against in a search engine to retrieve content that contains or is relevant to the term.

KEYWORD DENSITY: The use of a specific keyword present in any given piece of content. For example, given the keyword "racing" used five times in a 500-word blog post, the keyword density of "racing" would be 1%. Optimal keyword density is between 3 and 4%, and should not exceed 4% or it may be flagged as spamming.

KEYWORD PHRASE / LONG TAIL KEYWORD PHRASE: A phrase comprised of individual words but treated like a single keyword for the purposes of a search, like "Nascar car racing" or "racing opportunities in Texas".

KEYWORD RICH: Content that has many keywords and uses them often, with good keyword density.

KEYWORD TOOL: Tools created to help select optimal keywords for search engine marketing, like Google's Keyword Tool. They often contain information such as amount of searches for a particular keyword and other metrics that help ascertain how popular or prevalent a given keyword or keyword phrase may be.

LINKEDIN: A social networking site that is geared towards businesses and professionals, enabling them to link up and network more effectively.

LOCAL SEARCH RETURN: A feature within Google's search engine that returns location-specific results for a user who types in keywords that relate to local businesses. For example, a local search return would appear for a user in Omaha, Nebraska who typed in "Omaha Nebraska Homes For Sale." A map and local businesses that are relevant to the search result would appear in the ensuing search page.

NICHING: The practice of specializing your marketing strategy to a certain keyword or keyword phrase in order to rank in the highest spot in a local search return for that keyword or keyword phrase.

ROI: An acronym for "Return on Investment," which means the amount of profit; in literal terms, the amount of money returned for the amount of money invested.

SEARCH ALGORITHM: A series of computer algorithms used by major search engines to index, search, and rank websites on the Internet.

SEARCH ENGINE: A website or company, like Google, Bing, or Yahoo, that indexes other websites on the Internet and allows users to enter keywords in order to find relevant websites.

SEO: An acronym for "Search Engine Optimization." It refers to the section of marketing that tries to increase exposure and clientele by using techniques and strategies to rank high on Internet search engines. Often interchanged with SEM (Search Engine Marketing).

SOCIAL MEDIA: Sites whose primary purpose is to enable users to share content with each other and socialize on the Internet; examples of websites that fall into this category are Facebook, Twitter, and LinkedIn.

SPAM: In Internet parlance, spam was originally used to refer to any unsolicited bulk messages sent over email. It is now also commonly used to refer to content on the Internet which is not useful and designed to make a page rank higher on search engines by tricking search engine algorithms into rating the content as more useful than it actually is.

TWEET: An individual post on Twitter.

TWITTER: A social networking service that allows users to post 140-character tweets to their account, with the ability for other users to follow them and respond to the tweets.

UNIQUE SELLING POSITION (USP): Unique Selling Position separates you from your competition in a specific market place. The term is often used to refer to any aspect of an object that differentiates it from similar objects.

URL: An acronym for "Uniform Resource Locator". It is the name that the user types into the browser bar in order to access a specific website; for example, "www.google.com" or "www.bing.com" would be examples of URLs.

WORDPRESS: WordPress is a free and open source blogging tool and a content management system (CMS) based on PHP and MySQL, which runs on a web hosting service. Features include a plug-in architecture and a template system. WordPress is used by more than 18.9% of the top 10 million websites as of August 2013. WordPress is the most popular blogging system in use on the Web, at more than 60 million websites.

Made in the USA
Charleston, SC
29 April 2014